A GOODLY SHIP

PETER H. SPECTRE   DAVID LARKIN

A GOODLY SHIP

THE BUILDING OF THE SUSAN CONSTANT

Principal photography by Paul Rocheleau

Houghton Mifflin Company

Boston   New York   London   1992

A David Larkin Book

We would like to thank the following for
their help and cooperation in the preparation
of this book.

Maria Anderson, Kathleen Brandes, Maynard Bray,
Fred Brooks, Peter von Busch, Arne Emil Christensen,
Birthe Clausen, Joe Garland, Liz Gwillim, Sibylla Hasum,
Llewellyn Howland III, John Hudson, Eric Kentley,
Brian Lavery, Paul Lipke, Kenneth C. Martin, Hugh Messner,
James Moore, Allen and Liz Rawl, Mike Rines, David Spence, Eric Speth,
John Valliant, Jean de Vandière, and especially
Jon Wilson
and the folks at
WoodenBoat
Brooklin, Maine

The photographs are by Paul Rocheleau, except for those on the following pages:
Starke Jett, 87, 88/89, 90, 94/95; Allen Rawl, 27, 31, 35; Eric Speth, 73, 86, 91,
92, 93; K. Wetzel, 2/3, 64, 65, 68.

Printed in Hong Kong

For information about permission to reproduce selections from this book, write
to Permissions, Houghton Mifflin Company, 215 Park Avenue South, New
York, New York 10003.

CIP data available.
ISBN 0-395-57322-X

FCI   10   9   8   7   6   5   4   3   2   1

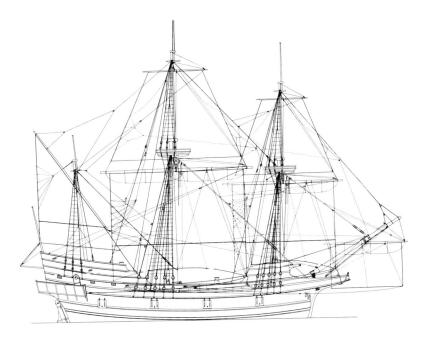

IN THE AFTERNOON of April 26, 1607, three tiny vessels entered Chesapeake Bay from the Atlantic Ocean and came to anchor near the mouth of what is now called the James River. They were the ships *Susan Constant* and *Godspeed* and the pinnace *Discovery*, under orders from the Virginia Company of London, 127 days out of England by way of the Canary Islands and the Caribbean.

The little ships were typical merchant traders of the beginning of the seventeenth century. The largest, the *Susan Constant*, was hardly bigger than a twentieth-century cruising yacht. The smallest, the *Discovery*, was not much larger than a lifeboat carried by one of today's luxury liners. The vessels were crowded with passengers and crew; their holds were packed to the deckbeams with provisions and supplies for an expedition that would have to be self-sufficient for months at a time, perhaps even years.

These little ships, cockleshells by today's standards, carried the core of what would become the Jamestown Settlement, the first successful permanent English colony in North America, which preceded the *Mayflower* landing and Plymouth Colony by thirteen years. The original settlers who survived and later immigrants would establish the Old Dominion of Virginia and lay the foundation for the English domination of North America at a time when it was thought the Spanish, who had had a vast head start, would inherit the continent.

A boat from the *Susan Constant* pushed off for the shore. "There wee landed," wrote George Percy, one of the colonists, "and discovered a little way . . . faire meddowes and goodly tall Trees, with such Fresh-waters running through the woods, as I almost ravished at the first sight thereof."

It had been a long voyage, almost four and a half months, in fair winds and foul, calms and violent storms, with seasickness, extreme discomfort, and death. Among the passengers and crew, even among the leaders, there had been endless disputes over the course to be taken and the appropriateness of the goal. Now, in the shelter of a peninsula jutting into Chesapeake Bay, in the gentle air of Tidewater Virginia in the spring, the men of the expedition strode the silver beaches, walked the woods, drank the pure waters, and thanked their lucky stars they were there and no longer on the heaving, lonely sea. They had survived an arduous voyage and found what they sought. They were eager to choose a site for their settlement and get on with living in a land so full of promise.

Tidewater Virginia may have seemed promising that first afternoon ashore, but in the evening, as a portent of things to come, there were strange cries in the woods. The men, fearing for their lives, hastened back to the boat on the beach. "When wee were going aboard," wrote Percy, "there came the Savages creeping upon all fours, from the Hills like Beares, with their Bowes in their mouthes."

The Jamestown Settlement, for all its fame, was not the first English colony in North America; rather, it was the first successful one. The Jamestown voyage had been preceded by a number of explorations by such Englishmen as John Cabot, Sebastian Cabot, and Bartholomew Gosnold, and by fishermen from the West Country of England who worked the banks off the Canadian Maritimes and New England. Martin Frobisher attemped a colony at Baffin Island as part of his search for a Northwest Passage; Sir Humphrey Gilbert tried the same thing on the coast of Newfoundland. In the late sixteenth century, Sir Walter Raleigh tried three times to set up a permanent colony on Roanoake Island, in what is now North Carolina. All failed.

The genesis of the Jamestown Settlement was the establishment of a small trading company a short time after the end of the Anglo-Spanish War, which ran from 1588 to 1604. A group of investors, seeing an opportunity for commercial gain in a period of peace, obtained a charter from King James I of England. Dated April 10, 1606, the charter in effect divided North America in half. The northern territory was reserved for petitioners from the cities of Bristol and Plymouth. The southern territory went to a joint-stock trading company known as the Virginia Company of London, of which there were seven principals: Sir Henry Montague and Sir William Wade, lawyers; Sir William Cope and Sir George Moore, both with close ties to King James's court; and Sir William Romney, Sir Thomas Smythe, and John Eldred, all involved with the giant East India Company.

A royal patent to half a continent! Straightaway, the Virginia Company of London announced its intention to start a colony in the heart of their chartered territory. The stated purposes were:

. . . first to preach and baptize into Christian Religion, and by propagation of the Gospell, to recover out of the Armes of the Divell, a number of Poore and miserable soules [i.e., save the Indians]. . . .

Secondly, to provide and build up for the publike Honour and Safety of our Gratious King and his Estates. . . .

Lastly, the appearance and assurance of Private commodity to the particular undertakers, by recovering and possessing to themselves a fruitfull land, whence they may furnish and provide this Kingdome, with all such necessities and defects (Copper, Iron, Steel, Timber for ships, yards, masts, cordage, sope ashes) under which we labor.

For all the noble intentions of the first two points, the last was the true operating principle. Commercial enterprise was, in fact, the primary function of the Virginia Company. Not only would great gain be realized, it was thought, by colonizing the New World, but also, with luck, explorers based at the settlement would find the fabled Northwest Passage to the unbelievable riches of the Far East.

But first a transatlantic expedition had to be organized — no mean feat in an era when it was difficult to plan for the future because the shape of the future was nearly impossible to discern. Money had to be raised, supplies purchased, and colonists recruited. Most important, transportation had to be arranged — ships, boats, and men to sail them.

The men of the Virginia Company were no fools. They recognized that there were two parts to the matter of choosing ships. Part one was to find deep-water vessels seaworthy enough to make the passage across the Atlantic. Part two was to arrange for coastal vessels suitable for extensive exploration of the shallow waters of Chesapeake Bay.

They settled on three vessels. Two were of great capacity and seaworthiness. The third had very little capacity and was barely large enough to make the ocean passage, but she was just the right size and draft for working her way through shoal waters and up narrow rivers and creeks. What's more, the Company arranged for a fourth vessel, a shallop — a sloop-rigged open boat — to be built in England and then knocked down for transport in one of the ships. Once in the New World, the shallop, perfect for coastal exploration and for carrying landing parties, would be put back together again.

Not counting the shallop, the smallest vessel, purchased especially for the voyage, was the pinnace *Discovery*, 20 tons burthen, commanded by John Ratcliffe. The next largest was the 40-ton *Godspeed*, leased from the Muscovy Company, which traded with Russia, and commanded by Bartholomew Gosnold. The largest — twice the size of the other two put together — was the *Susan Constant*, 120 tons burthen. She was commanded by Captain Christopher Newport, after whom Newport News would be named, and was leased from the firm of Colthurst, Dapper, Wheatley and Company of London. (The merchant Wheatley was involved in the sale of masts and deal boards. He would have had a great interest in the Jamestown expedition, as timber was expected to be one of the main exports from Virginia.)

The *Susan Constant* was the flagship of the squadron, and a famous ship in historical terms, yet few specifics are known about her. Nothing about who built her or where she was built, her precise dimensions, the color of her decorations or whether she had any decorations at all, and the shape of her hull.

All that is known is that about a month before the *Susan Constant* set sail for Virginia, she was involved in a collision with a smaller vessel, the *Philip and Francis*, in the Thames River just below London. The accident caused minor damage, but it was enough, nevertheless, to involve her owners in a lawsuit. It is from this suit that the size of the *Susan Constant* has been determined. Depositions in the case included statements that the ship was registered in London, that she was only about a year old ("The buildinge thereof which ys aboute a yeare past"), that she had traded with Spain, and that she was about 120 tons burthen ("The *Susan Constant* is of the burthen of one hundreth and twenty tonnes or thereabouts").

Tons burthen, or burden, referred to the amount of cargo a ship could carry and was the then-standard way to describe a vessel. Ferdinand Magellan's *Trinidada,* for example, was described as being of 110 tons burthen. She was said to have been of 200 tons displacement — that is, her hull displaced 200 tons of water — and measured 78 feet on the waterline, 22½ feet beam at the waterline, and had a mean draft, or depth, when loaded of 8 feet.

Naval architects and historians, taking into consideration what they know about merchant trading ships of the period, and assuming that the *Susan Constant* was a typical medium-sized vessel, have interpreted the 120-ton-burthen figure to mean she must have been about 55 feet length of keel, 96 feet length of hull, 23 feet width, and 9½ feet depth of hold.

Considering that the *Susan Constant* was registered in the port of London, most historians speculate she must have been built at one of the several shipyards operating on the banks of the Thames in the vicinity of London. Yards such as these had been constructing wooden ships for years, and the men who worked in them — ships's carpenters, plankers, sawyers, caulkers, sparmakers — could draw on generations of tradition and experience.

The most important asset of the typical shipyard of the period was the land it sat on, as the working facilities themselves would have been limited. The land would be clear, sloping gradually to the water, with a few insubstantial buildings for housing a woodworking shop, a rigging and sail loft, a shipsmith's forge, and storage for tools and supplies. Most of the work was done right out in the open. There would be a sawpit for sawing out planks by hand, a slipway for launching vessels, a framing platform for getting out sawn frames, sheerlegs for lifting heavy objects, a mast yard for making spars, a storage yard for raw timbers, and not much more.

The basic methods used for building ships like the *Susan Constant* were centuries old and would continue to be used for centuries to come. Virtually the only things a skilled wooden shipwright of today might miss in a seventeenth-century shipyard are power tools and a few materials that were then unavailable. Even the terms used to describe the processes of building and the parts of a vessel remain more or less the same.

The design of the ships, however, was quite different. To modern eyes, vessels like the *Susan Constant* seem topheavy and clunky, almost primitive when compared to the mighty clipper ships of two and a half centuries later and the yachts of today, but even so, their design, like their construction, was the result of careful consideration and years of experience. Here is what Sir Henry Mainwaring wrote about proper ship design of that period in *The Seaman's Dictionary:*

The bow is of great importance for this first breaks the sea and is that part which bears all the ship forward on when she is pressed down with sail, which is in a manner the bearing of the ship. If the bow be too broad the ship will not pass easily through the sea but carry a great deal of dead water before her; if it be too lean or thin, she will pitch or beat mightily into a hollow sea for want of breadth to bear her up, so that there must be a discreet mean betwixt both these. The shaping of this part doth much import the ship's going by a wind; yet I have seen both sorts go well by a wind, but most commonly those have good bold bows; nevertheless it is certain that a ship's way after on — which is called her run — is of more importance for her sailing by a wind. The run is of main importance for the ship's sailing, for if the water come not swiftly to the rudder she will never steer well, and it is a general observation that a ship that doth not steer well will not sail well, and then she cannot keep a good wind, for if a ship hath not fresh way through the sea she must needs fall to leeward with the sea. We say a ship hath a good run when it is long and cometh off handsomely by degrees, and a bad run when it is short and that the ship is too full below.

"On Saturday, the twentieth of December in the yeere 1606," wrote George Percy, who kept an account of the voyage, "the fleet fell from London." Though it was a cold damp day and the heart of the winter was yet before them, the three vessels, plus the knocked-down shallop, got under way with a favorable tide and sailed down the Thames to the sea.

Conditions aboard all the vessels were unbelievably cramped. There were, of course, the passengers and crews: the *Susan Constant* carried 71 men; the *Godspeed*, 52; the tiny *Discovery*, 21. Then there were the provisions and water for the voyage and the material required for the operation of the ships. They carried cargo, tools, clothing, food, and other supplies to be landed with the colonists in Virginia, even livestock for both fresh meat and milk at sea and for farming in the new land. No list survives of the possessions the original colonists took with them, but here are excerpts of a list from a later voyage, in the 1620s:

Apparell for one man
One Monmouth Cap
Three shirts
One Waste-coate
One sute of Canvase
One sute of Frize
One sute of Cloth
Three pair of Irish stockins
Foure paire of shooes
One paire of garters
One paire of Canvase sheets
Seven Ells of Canvase, to make a bed and boulster, to be filled in Virginia
One rug for a bed serving for two men
Five Ells coorse Canvase, to make a bed at Sea for two men, to be filled with straw
One coorse Rug at Sea for two men

Victuall for a whole yeere for one man
Eight bushels of Meale
Two bushels of Pease
Two bushels of Oatmeale
One gallon of Aquavitae
One gallon of Oyle
Two gallons of Vinegar

Armes for one man
One Armour, compleat, light
One long Piece, five foot or five and a halfe, neere Musket bore
One Sword
One Belt
One Bandaleere
Twentie pound of Powder
Sixtie pound of shot or lead, Pistoll and Goose shot

Tooles for a Family of sixe persons
Five broad howes [hoes]
Five narrow howes
Two broad Axes
Five felling Axes
Two Steele Hand-sawes
Two two-hand-saws
One whip-saw, set and filed with boxe, file and wrest
Two hammers
Three shovels
Two Spades
Two Augers
Six Chissels
Two percers [awls]
Three gimblets
Two hatchets
Two froves [froes]
Two hand-bils
One Grindlestone
Nailes of all sorts
Two Pickaxes

Household Implements for a Family of six persons
One Iron Pot
One Kettle
One large frying-pan
One Griddiron
Two Skillets
One Spit
Platters, dishes, Spoones of wood

In the best of conditions there was hardly enough room aboard ship for turning around, but in rough weather . . . Well, imagine a closet without enough headroom for standing up straight, packed with boxes, bales, rope, hammocks, and assorted gear.

Fill the spaces between with people who haven't been able to take a bath for weeks. Imagine the closet tossing and turning in a heavy seaway. Make the atmosphere damp and cold. Put the fear of the unknown in the minds of the occupants. Now you have a mild approximation of what it was like to be aboard any one of the ships of the squadron.

Keeping order in conditions like that was no easy task. It would have been difficult enough if one person had the authority of command, but as it was there were several, the captains of the individual ships: Bartholomew Gosnold, John Ratcliffe, and Christopher Newport, who as captain of the *Susan Constant* was also leader of the squadron and carried the operational orders issued by the Virginia Company. (Both Gosnold and Newport had had considerable experience in North American waters and were familiar with the coast of Virginia.)

The crew of each vessel had their own organization. Besides the captain, there were four principal officers aboard the *Susan Constant:* the master, who was in charge of sailing the veessel; the pilot, who navigated within sight of shore; the navigator, who set the course on the open sea; and the ship's carpenter, who looked after the physical well-being of the vessel. The cook, the sailmaker, the rigger, the seamen, and others filled out the rest of the crew.

And then there were the leaders of the colonists: Edward Maria Wingfield, an experienced soldier of genteel background, who would be elected president of the governing council when the colonists became established in Virginia; George Kendall, known for his political connections; Captain John Smith, also an experienced soldier; and John Martin, a mariner.

No wonder the voyage was marked by disagreement, especially among the leadership! Hotheadedness may not have prevailed at all times, but it certainly wasn't uncommon. Before the squadron reached Virginia, Captain Smith, for example, was put in confinement after several arguments with other gentlemen of the expedition.

In 1606, the weather in England at the end of December was as poor as it ever has been. No sooner did the fleet reach the mouth of the Thames than it was struck by contrary winds and storms. "The fift of January we anchored in the Downes," George Percy wrote in his journal, "but the winds continued contrarie so long, that we were forced to stay there some time, where wee suffered great stormes, but by the skilfulnesse of the Captaine wee suffered no great losse or danger."

The fleet remained within sight of England for six weeks, much of the time at anchor, but finally they were blessed with fair winds and made their way to the Canary Islands to take on fresh water. Theirs was the classical trade-winds passage, guided by the old English mariners' rule of thumb, "South 'til the butter melts, then west" — a downwind romp under sunny skies, billowing clouds, and in relatively warm temperatures, with only the occasional storm, to the West Indies.

"The three and Twentieth day [of February]," Percy wrote, "we fell withe the Iland of Mattanenio]Martinique] in the West Indies." To say the ships' companies were delighted to reach solid land would be an understatement. The men visited the Caribbean islands with joy and thanksgiving, remaining there for several weeks, sailing from island to island. They rested, replenished their provisions, explored, stretched their legs ashore, traded with the natives, and gathered themselves for the last leg of the voyage.

"The tenth day [of April]," wrote Percy, "we set saile, and disimboged out of the West Indies, and bare our course Northerly." They crossed the Tropic of Cancer on the fourteenth, enjoying fine sailing weather, but it was not to continue. "The one and twentieth day [of April], about five a clocke at night there began a vehement tempest, which lasted all the night, with winds, raine, and thunders in terrible manner. Wee were forced to lie at Hull that night, because we thought wee had beene nearer land than wee were."

Indeed, they were not. They sounded for the depth of water with a lead line and found no bottom. They were far off shore — "off soundings" in the terminology of the mariner — to the east and south of their intended landfall, the capes of Virginia that define the mouth of Chesapeake Bay. But they found increasingly positive signs of land the farther they sailed, until finally, with great rejoicing, they spied the capes. "The six and twentieth day of Aprill," Percy wrote, "about foure a clocke in the morning, wee descried the Land of Virginia: the same day wee entred into the Bay of Chesupioc directly, without any let or hindrance."

The sea voyage was over. Now the exploration of the lower end of the Chesapeake would begin. The goal, as outlined in the detailed instructions provided by the Virginia Company, was to find an appropriate site for a colony. "When it Shall please God to Send you on the Coast of Virginia," the orders said, "you shall Do your best Endeavour to find out a Safe port in the Entrance of Some navigable River making Choise of Such as one as runneth furthest into the Land. And if you happen to Discover Divers portable Rivers and amongst them any one that hath two main branches if the Difference be not Great make Choise of that which bendeth most towards the Northwest for that way shall You soonest find the Other Sea." The "Other Sea" referred to here is the Pacific Ocean. European explorers still believed that the East Coast of North America was connected to the West Coast by a Northwest Passage through the heart of the continent.

The very next day, April 27, the ships' carpenters began assembling the shallop. The *Susan Constant* and the *Godspeed* would explore the deeper waters and the channels of the bay; the *Discovery* and the shallop would work the shoals, rivers, and creeks. They were at it for more than two weeks, as the shoreline of Chesapeake Bay was as convoluted as any coast the sailors of the fleet had ever seen. One minute they would be in water deep enough to float even the *Susan Constant*. The next, they would be over shoals of danger even to the shallop. Everywhere they went, they left a name as a remembrance of their experience there.

Old Point Comfort: "Wee rowed over to a point of Land, where wee found a channell, and sounded six, eight, ten, or twelve fathom: which put us in good comfort. Therefore wee named that point of Land, Cape Comfort."

Cape Henry: "The nine and twentieth day [of April] we set up a Cross at Chesupioc Bay, and named that place Cape Henry."

Archers Hope: "The twelfth day [of May] we went backe to our ships, and discovered a point of Land, called Archers Hope [after one of the gentlemen of the expedition].

On May 13, 1607, they found their spot, a small island on the north bank of the James, a few miles upriver from the mouth, "where our shippes do lie so neere the shoare that they are moored to the Trees in six fathoms of water." It seemed like the perfect place for a settlement, at least on first inspection.

"This River which wee have discovered," wrote George Percy in a blaze of enthusiasm, "is one of the famousest Rivers that ever was found by any Christian, it ebbes and flowes a hundred and threescore miles where ships of great burthen may harbour in saftie. Wheresoever we landed up this River, we saw goodliest Woods as Beech, Oke, Cedar, Cypresse, Wal-nuts, Sassafras and Vines in great abundance, which hang in great clusters on many Trees, and other Trees unknowne, and all the grounds bespred with many sweet and delicate flowres of divers colours and kindes. There are also many fruites as Strawberries, Mulberries, Rasberries and Fruits unknowne, there are many branches of this River, which runne flowing through the Woods with great plentie of fish of all kindes, as for Sturgeon all the World cannot be compared to it. In the Countrey I have seene many great and large Meadowes having excellent good pasture for any Cattle. There are Beares, Foxes, Otters, Bevers, Muskats, and wild beasts unknowne."

Later, when reality set in, Percy and his compatriots were a little less enthusiastic. Yes, the site for Jamestown had deep water, and yes, it was easily defended, and yes, there was abundant game for food and great stands of trees from which to cut lumber for housing. But much of the island was marshy, making it a breeding ground for mosquitoes; there were no fresh-water springs on the island itself, and the river water was brackish; and the territory belonged to a tribe of Indians that tended to be antagonistic more often than friendly.

But none of that deterred the colonists. They were happy to have finally picked a site and were eager to get established. Their instructions from the Virginia Company were explicit: "When you have Discovered as far up the River as you mean to plant Your Selves and Landed your victuals and munitions to the End that Every man may know his Charge you Shall Do well to Divide your Six Score men into three parts whereof one forty of them you may appoint to fortifie and build of which your first work must be your Storehouse for Victual 30 Others you may imploy in preparing your Ground and Sowing your Corn and Roots the Other ten of these forty you must Leave as Sentinel at the havens mouth The Other forty you may imploy for two Months in Discovery of the River above you and on the Contry about you which Charge Captain Newport and Captain Gosnold may undertake."

And that is what they did. They named their river the James and their settlement Jamestown ("We proclaimed James King of England to have the most right unto it"). They hauled their provisions, tools, and personal belongings ashore and began building a little village, which, though crude, would be sufficient. "Wee did hang an awning (which is an old Saile) to three or foure trees to shadow us from the Sunne," wrote Captain John Smith. "Our walles were rales of wood, our seats unhewed trees till we cut plankes, our Pulpit a bar of wood nailed to two neighboring trees. In foule weather we shifted into an old rotten tent."

The names of these first settlers, the men who built Jamestown, were recorded by Captain Smith:

Councell
Maister Edward Maria Wingfield
Captaine Bartholomew Gosnoll
Captaine John Smyth
Captaine John Ratliffe
Captaine John Martin
Captaine George Kendall

Gentlemen
Maister Robert Hunt, Preacher
Maister George Percie
Anthony Gosnoll
Captaine Gabriell Archer
Robert Ford
William Bruster
Dru Pickhouse
John Brookes
Thomas Sands
John Robinson
Ustis Clovill
Kellam Throgmorton
Nathaniell Powell
Robert Behethland
Jeremy Alicock
Thomas Studley
Richard Crofts
Nicholas Houlgrave

Thomas Webbe
John Waler
William Tankard
Francis Snarsbrough
Edward Brookes
Richard Dixon
John Martin
George Martin
Anthony Gosnold
Thomas Wotton, Sierg. [Surgeon]
Thomas Gore
Francis Midwinter

Carpenters
William Laxon
Edward Pising
Thomas Emry
Robert Small

Others
Anas Todkill
John Capper
James Read, Blacksmith
Jonas Profit, Sailer
Thomas Couper, Barber

John Herd, Bricklayer
Edward Brinto, Mason
William Love, Taylor
Nicholas Skot, Drummer

Labourers
John Laydon
William Cassen
George Cassen
Thomas Cassen
William Rods
William White
Ould Edward
Henry Tavin
George Golding
John Dods
William Johnson
William Unger
William Wilkinson, Surgeon

Boys
Samuell Collier
Nathaniel Pecock
James Brumfield
Richard Mutton

In fact, John Smith wasn't a member of the council, even though he had been chosen for it by the Virginia Company before the expedition set sail. A man of action and strong opinion, Smith was at first disliked and distrusted by his compatriots. After having been put in confinement aboard the *Susan Constant,* and after continuing to argue with the other leaders about the proper course of action, he was banned from the council by Edward Maria Wingfield. Later, in the colony's darkest hours, it was Smith who would be saved from death by the Indian maiden Pocahontas, and who would, through the force of his personality, save Jamestown from Indian attacks, starvation, and ruin.

With the storerooms and rudimentary housing complete, the settlers built a fort to defend themselves from the Indians, as well as from the Spaniards if the time should come when Spain might dispute England's tiny foothold in North America. And then, on June 22, when all was done that could be done, the *Susan Constant* and the *Godspeed,* the settlement's primary means of contact with the civilized world, got under way.

The two ships, flags and pennants flying from their mastheads, sailed down the James River, through Hampton Roads, between the Virginia capes, and out into the Atlantic Ocean. They were bound for London, from which they would never return, as the colony would be resupplied by other ships at other times. They left behind the little *Discovery* and the shallop, and a group of men who would suffer attacks from Indians, disease, starvation, and death. The survivors, nevertheless, would persevere.

And what would become of the *Susan Constant?* After she returned to London, her charter to the Virginia Company expired, and she went back to general trading around the British Isles and in European waters. She is known to have made a voyage from Bristol to Marseilles, and there are reports of her being involved in a case of piracy in 1618, though there is some speculation that the *Susan Constant* may have been a different ship of the same name. Nothing more is known. Our ship lived out her days and then disappeared into the mists of time.

In April 1957, to commemorate the 350th anniversary of the founding of Jamestown, the Jamestown Festival Park opened near the original site of the colony. Besides exhibits depicting the houses, occupations, and lives of the colonists, as well as a typical Indian village, the park also has a permanent waterfront display. For this, full-scale reproductions of the *Susan Constant,* the *Godspeed,* and the *Discovery* were built. Over the years, thousands of people have visited the park, as much to see this unique collection of colonial vessels as to see the land-bound exhibits.

Time took its toll on the little ships, however, and by the 1980s all three were due for replacement. New reproductions of the *Godspeed* and the *Discovery* were launched in 1984. In early 1985 the new *Godspeed* was shipped by freighter to England and then was sailed from London on April 30 to reenact the original voyage of 1607. She returned to the Jamestown Festival Park in late October.

Meanwhile, significant advances in historical research and, especially, underwater archaeology had been made regarding colonial ships. More was known about the *Susan Constant* than ever before, and so the new reproduction would be based on the latest scholarship. Not only would there be a new *Susan Constant,* but she would also be as historically accurate as possible.

A master shipbuilder who had worked on several other historical reproductions was engaged to build the ship. A crew of experienced shipwrights was put together, a shop was erected, building stocks were set up, and the keel of the vessel was laid in December 1989 at the Jamestown Settlement, as it is now known, on the bank of the James River. For more than a year, visitors to the settlement were treated to the sights and sounds of an unfolding drama — the building of a wooden ship.

> *Build me straight, O worthy Master!*
> *Stanch and strong, a goodly vessel,*
> *That shall laugh at all disaster,*
> *And with wave and whirlwind wrestle!*
>
> "The Building of the Ship," 1849,
> HENRY WADSWORTH LONGFELLOW

THE BUILDING OF THE SUSAN CONSTANT

And first with nicest skill and art,
Perfect and finished in every part,
A little model, the Master wrought,
Which should be to the larger plan
What the child is to the man,

Its counterpart in miniature;
That with a hand more swift and sure
The greater labor might be brought
To answer to his inward thought.

Until a century or so ago, ships and boats were not designed on paper as they are now. The designer, who usually was also the builder, would consult with the future owner to determine the requirements of the vessel — its use, its size, the accommodations for the crew, the stowage capacity, and so forth. The designer would then carve a scale half model of the hull from a solid block of wood, or from a block made of several layers of wood pinned together, incorporating into it those shapes he knew from experience would produce the required characteristics: long and lean for speed, wide and deep for cargo-carrying ability, whatever the owner desired. This model would be of only half the hull — hence the term *builder's half hull model* — on the assumption that a hull cut in half longitudinally would be shaped the same, a mirror image, on both sides.

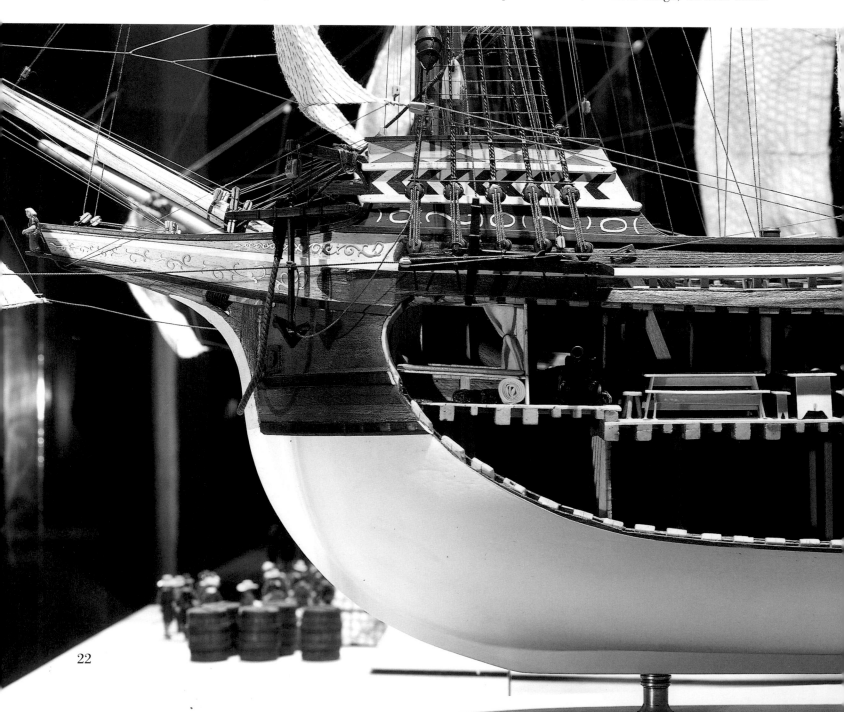

Once the designer was satisfied with the shape, and the owner concurred, the builder would take the lines of the hull off the half hull model, using various measuring devices, and draw them full size on a lofting floor — a flat, open space with a smooth surface. From these lines, which delineated in two dimensions the three-dimensional form of the hull, he would make patterns of thin wood for the principal parts: the stem, the stern, the individual frames, and so on. He would then use the patterns for drawing out the shapes of the parts on the rough timbers.

The half hull model, a working tool, was seldom used for decoration. For display purposes — perhaps as a centerpiece in the shipowner's office or home, or as a sales tool to convince wealthy backers to invest in the construction of a ship — the owner sometimes had a more elaborate model built, rigged as the vessel would be when finished. Today, in the absence of the vessels themselves, fully rigged models are built to show the details of ships of the past. Here we have a very elaborate model of the *Susan Constant*, cut away along the side to reveal the interior of the vessel.

Thus with the rising of the sun
Was the noble task begun,
And soon throughout the ship-yard's bounds
Were heard the intermingled sounds
Of axes and of mallets, plied
With vigorous arms on every side;
Plied so deftly and so well,
That, ere the shadows of evening fell,
The keel of oak for a noble ship,
Scarfed and bolted, straight and strong,
Was lying ready, and stretched along
The blocks, well placed upon the slip.

Wooden hulls are subjected to several types of strains produced by such forces as the action of the sea, the effects of propulsion, and the weight of the vessel. Some of these strains are longitudinal, some transverse, and others are localized.

The backbone is the foundation of the vessel. Its shape determines the profile of the hull, and its structure provides considerable resistance to longitudinal and localized strains. In addition, it assists the frames and other members in resisting transverse strains. The backbone consists of three sections — the stem, the sternpost, and the keel — each made of several individual parts fastened together. The keel of the *Susan Constant* is greenheart, a tropical hardwood, noted for its strength, density, and resistance to rot.

Once the backbone has been assembled, it is set up on the building stocks, aligned, and braced.

The hull of the *Susan Constant* is a complex shape, wide in the middle and narrowing toward the ends, so a cross section of the hull at any given point along her length will be different from any other. The frames, which in effect represent cross sections, are therefore all unique in shape.

Choose the timbers with greatest care;
Of all that is unsound beware;
For only what is sound and strong
To this vessel shall belong.

Each frame is built separately, to its own complex pattern, of several pieces of wood — the *Susan Constant*'s are of such tropical hardwoods as mora, purpleheart, and courbaril — cut to shape according to patterns determined by the master builder. All of these pieces need to be curved to a greater or lesser extent, so they are sawn from crooked wood with sweeping grain. The frame maker matches the sweep of the curve to the sweep of the grain, producing a timber that retains the natural strength of the tree from which it came.

This is what is known as double-sawn construction — each frame made in two layers, each section with its own name. There are floor timbers (the lower section of the frame that crosses the keel), futtocks, and top timbers, the topmost parts of the frame on each side. The individual pieces of the frame are cut according to the master builder's pattern, beveled on the edges to follow the run of the planking, and then assembled into the whole on a framing platform specially built for the task. Hundreds of individual pieces are used to construct the vast number of frames in the *Susan Constant*, and each piece must be systematically numbered and checked.

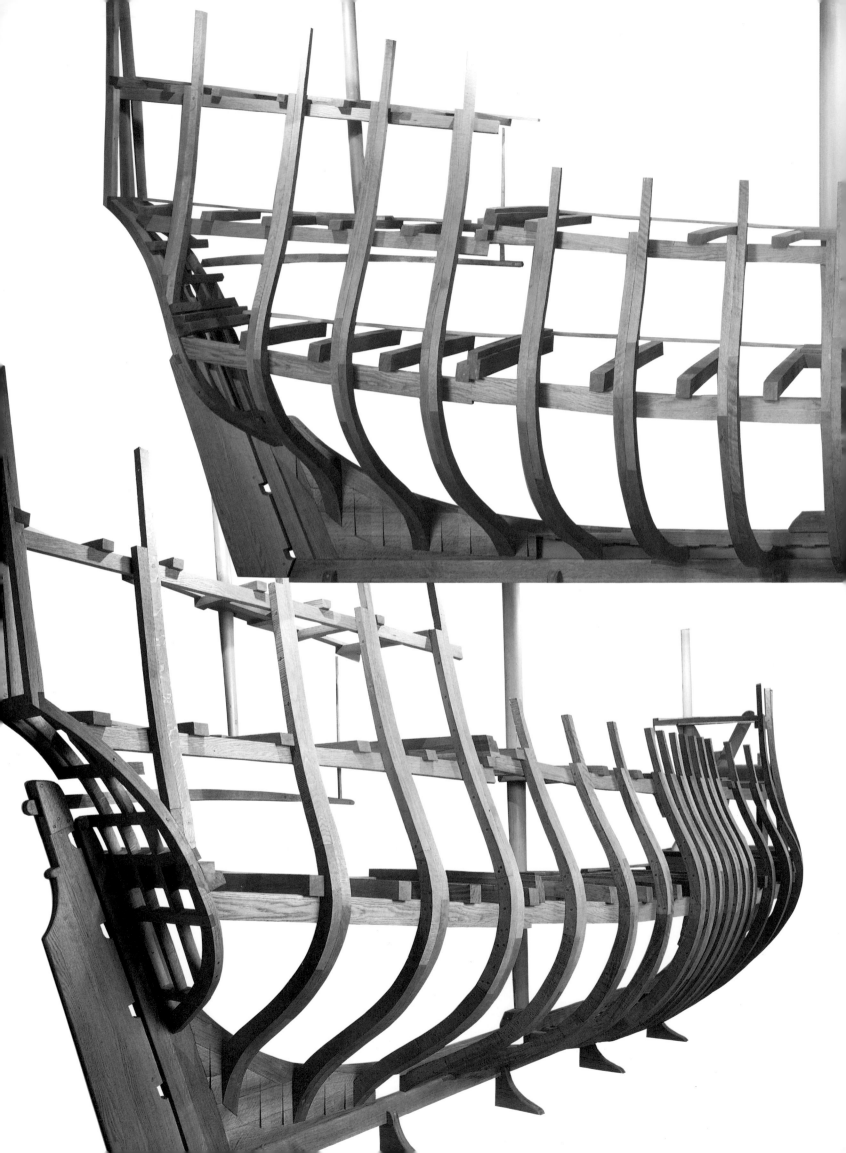

The backbone, with about half the frames and deckbeams in place, and the bowsprit, masts, rudder, and tiller rigged. The cluster of seven frames in the middle shows the eventual frame spacing when the hull is finished.

Tar is spread between the pieces of the frame to prevent moisture from seeping into the seams and causing rot, and they are fastened together with trunnels. Moisture, especially fresh water, is the great enemy of wooden ships. If it is allowed to settle into cracks and crevices in the wood and gaps in joints between wooden members, and if the temperature is warm enough, rot-producing organisms can grow and spread.

left

Although metal fastenings are used throughout the ship, wooden trunnels — "treenails," thick dowls — are used as well. A hole is drilled through the members to be joined with an auger, a tight-fitting trunnel is driven with a maul to fasten the pieces together, and the head of the trunnel is sawn off. Hardwood wedges are then driven into the ends of the trunnel to lock it securely in the hole. A properly driven trunnel is every bit as effective as a metal fastening — in some cases, more so.

right, top

The first frame has been erected, and the shipwrights are fitting temporary braces to prevent it from shifting. Earlier, the frame-making crew nailed temporary crosspieces, known as cross spalls, to the frame to keep it from spreading at the top. This view is from the after end of the backbone, looking forward. The darker-colored wood marks the backbone and frame; the lighter wood is that of the bracing.

right, bottom

This view is from the forward end of the backbone, looking aft. The frame was hauled upright by a pair of sheerlegs — a simple, crude, cranelike structure built on site by the yard crew. A block-and-tackle arrangement attached to the sternpost holds the sheerlegs upright. Another block-and-tackle attached to the forward side of the sheerlegs was used to pull the frame upright, its bottom resting on the keel. This is an ancient method for raising large, heavy timbers — surprisingly easy due to its carefully worked-out mechanical advantage.

The frames are erected, one after another, as quickly as they are constructed on the framing platform. The position of each frame is checked carefully, as any misalignment could result in crookedness or unfairness in the hull. Once the shipwrights are satisfied that everything is as it should be, they nail temporary cleats, short pieces of wood, to the inside and outside edges of the frames to keep them from shifting in relation to each other and to the keel. Side braces, or shores, are added to keep the framework from tilting to one side or the other. In the foreground is the framing platform, which has been constructed just forward of the hull. It is a temporary structure that will be removed after the framing is completed.

The ship in the background, moored to a pier that juts into the James River, is a reproduction of the colonial ship *Godspeed*.

The *Susan Constant*'s frames are closely spaced, but, because she is primarily a merchant vessel, not nearly as closely spaced as were those of wooden warships. The latter were heavily constructed, with massive frames and very little space between them — on the largest, the most powerful vessels, there was virtually no space at all — both to handle the weight of their armament and to act as a defense against the force of the enemy's cannonballs. The pile of timbers in the foreground contains offcuts from the frame-making process. The wood will not go to waste, however. Most will be used to fashion shorter members in the ship. The scrap will be used to fuel the shop stove during the cold-weather months.

above

Whole frames are used along most of the length of the hull, but in the after section, in the vicinity of the deadwood, they must be erected in halves because of the extreme depth of the deadwood. The deadwood is in effect a huge knee that reinforces the sternpost, the vertical member at the after end of the keel that supports the stern structure and the rudder. The deadwood is built up from several individual pieces of timber pinned together and fastened both to the keel and to the sternpost.

left

Using mallets and chisels, the shipwrights hew shallow mortises (sockets) in the sides of the deadwood to take the heels of the half frames, which must be cut to a precise angle so they align properly with the backbone. The half frames are erected in matching pairs — one on one side of the hull, its mirror image on the other side.

The backbone has been painted with red primer to protect the wood from drying too much during construction and developing checks, or cracks.

35

The skeleton of the ship emerges. The full frames of the midbody of the hull have been set up, and the yard crew has begun to work on the stern framing (the view here is from forward, looking aft). The two curved timbers on either side of the sternpost are the fashion timbers, which define the edge of the counter, or stern, of the vessel. They will be spanned by the transom timbers, crosswise members that further support the counter.

Before the half frames can be erected, they must be dragged aft along the keel: The framing platform is at the forward end of the construction ways. This may not be a full frame, but it still is quite heavy, weighing several hundred pounds. Here, two shipwrights are using a block-and-tackle to make the job easier. Note the extreme bevel at the heel of the frame, where it will be fit into its corresponding socket cut into the deadwood.

Spring has arrived in Jamestown, and the yard crew has prepared the site for the change in weather. The furled tarpaulin along the ridgepole running the length of the hull will be unrolled over the temporary rafters to keep spring rains and the hot sun of summer off the vessel.

The framing of the after end of the vessel has been completed. The heel of each of the half frames has been set in the heel sockets and fastened to the deadwood with metal spikes. The heads of the fastenings have been driven below the surface of the frames so they won't interfere with the planking.

right

The stem, like the backbone at the stern, is built of several members bolted together, with tar in the joints. Painted with red primer to prevent the wood from checking, it has been braced securely to keep it from shifting.

As the shipwrights prepare the last few forward frames, another yard crew constructs scaffolding around the hull for the plankers.

The little tree lashed to the top of the stem was put there by the shipwrights to celebrate their progress. It symbolizes the living nature of a wooden ship.

Day by day the vessel grew,
With timbers fashioned strong and true,
Stemson and keelson and steerson-knee,
Till, framed with perfect symmetry,
A skeleton ship rose up to view!

As at the stern, the frames at the bow are erected in halves. The foremost pairs are known as cant frames, because they are not erected square to the keel like the midbody frames but, due to the shape of the bow, canted forward.

left

Visible here are the heads of the bolts that fasten together the various pieces of the stem. The temporary cleats nailed to the inside of the stem are used as steps by the shipwrights. The short vertical timbers between the cant frames and the stem are fillers known as hawsepieces.

The completely framed-out hull, yet to be fitted with stringers, deckbeams, and planking, resembles a skeleton. The top timbers of the frames have been cut approximately to length; later, the shipwrights will trim them evenly to a curving sheerline determined by the planking boss.

And around the bows and along the side
The heavy hammers and mallets plied,
Till after many a week, at length,
Wonderful for form and strength,
Sublime in its enormous bulk,
Loomed aloft the shadowy hulk!

The frames hold the shape of the hull, but to add to the strength of the whole, they must be tied together with permanent members running the length of the vessel and complementing the work of the keel. Several of these longitudinals are fastened to the inside of the hull. Their importance cannot be overestimated.

Without them, the hull, over time, is likely to sag in the middle or droop at the ends. (The latter condition is known as hogging.) Long, thick timbers, or sleepers, are bent in from stem to stern between the keel and the top of the frames, and clamped securely. They are then fastened down with long metal spikes.

Another longitudinal member, the keelson, is laid over the frames, along the top of the keel, in effect creating a complementary interior keel. Long fastenings are driven through the keelson and the frames, down into the main keel, tying together all three structures. Long, thick timbers, or stringers, are bent in from stem to stern between the keel and the tops of the frames, and clamped securely. They are then fastened down with long metal spikes. In the development of wooden shipbuilding technology, the keelson proved to be one of the most important structural members in ship construction. As years passed and new vessels became longer and longer, the longitudinal strength of hulls had to be enhanced. Keelsons became wider and thicker, and were eventually doubled, tripled, and more, with "sister" keelsons.

The stringers fastened to the interiors of the frames serve triple duty: They tie the frames together, provide significant longitudinal strength to the hull, and serve as shelves to support the ends of the deckbeams. (The topmost stringer, the one on which the beam end actually rests, is called the clamp.) With the frames, stringers, and deckbeams locked together with metal fastenings, the basic interior framework of the hull is completed.

right

Like a post-and-beam building, the framed hull with the deckbeams in place has the appearance of an interlocking puzzle, with each piece contributing to the strength of the whole. In the absence of a science of structural engineering, the old-time shipwrights learned how to build ships that would stay together in all conditions by trial and error.

60

The *Susan Constant*'s deck framing not only provides a firm foundation for the deck planking, which will be laid longitudinally, but also adds strength to the entire structure of the vessel. The crosswise timbers, those running from side to side, are the deckbeams. They have camber — that is, they are curved so water can drain over the side. The short timbers between the deckbeams, running fore-and-aft, are carlins. The hewn timbers up in the bow, fastened to the stem, the cant frames, and the hawsepieces, are the breasthooks. They tie the deck framing to the stem while reinforcing the bow framing. The four holes on either side of the stem below the deck framing are hawseholes for the anchor cable.

Framers and plankers are not the only craftsmen working on the *Susan Constant*. In addition, there are the sailmakers, sparmakers, riggers, carvers, shipsmiths, and others.

above
The tools of the modern sailmaker differ little from those of centuries ago: special needles, triangular in cross section, with sharp edges to cut easily into the heavy sailcloth; leather sailmaker's palms, specially shaped to the user's hand, for pushing the needle into the cloth; fids and marlinspikes — long, pointed tools — of various sizes for working rope; punches for making grommet holes; seam rubbers for smoothing out the seams; and more. Today the long seaming is done with sewing machines, but the rest of the work is still done by hand.

The *Susan Constant* will set six individual sails — one on the mizzenmast, two each on the mainmast and foremast, and one on the bowsprit — for a total sail area of slightly more than 3,900 square feet. Here, a sailmaker is sewing a boltrope to a sail to reinforce the edge. In the past, canvas was of cotton or flax. Today, the *Susan Constant*'s sails are of Duradon, a synthetic fiber that looks and feels like traditional canvas but is stronger and lasts longer.

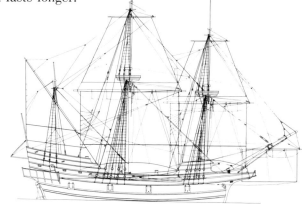

As a common workaday merchant vessel, the original *Susan Constant* was plainly decorated, though she no doubt had a carving here and there as appropriate. Here, two craftsmen work on the catheads, timbers projecting from either side of the bow; they are used to raise the anchors clear of the bow when the ship gets under way.

right

The rigging of sailing vessels requires a vast number of blocks and deadeyes. Blocks, which consist of a wooden shell holding a pulley that revolves around a pin, are used in various combinations with rope to improve mechanical advantage. Deadeyes, on the other hand, are blocks without a pulley, thick discs of wood with holes drilled in them. (They are, in effect, dead blocks with eyes — hence the name *deadeye*.) Lanyards, pieces of line, are run through the eyes for setting up the standing rigging. Here, a blockmaker is shaping a deadeye.

The planking of the hull is a long, tedious process. It is relatively straightforward at the after section of the hull and along the midsection, but quite difficult in the bows (where the planks take a tight curve) and near the keel (where they must bend and twist at the same time). Planks that have to take sharp bends must be steamed in a steam box to make them pliable.

The master builder and boss planker begin the process by lining out the planking, determining the exact location of each strake or line of plank, and marking the widths. Although a finished hull may look as if it has been planked with straight-edged strakes of uniform width, such is not the case. Rather, the strakes vary in width to accommodate the varying fullness of the hull along its length. The proper dimensions are laid out on the rough planking stock and sawed to shape.

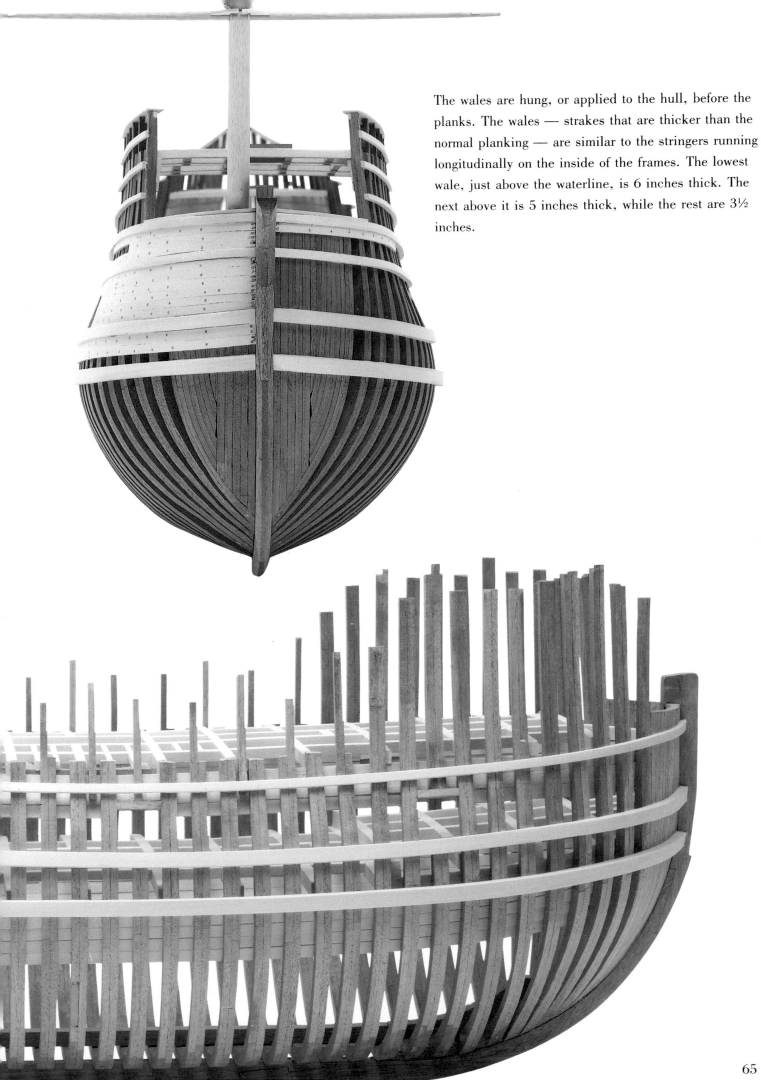

The wales are hung, or applied to the hull, before the planks. The wales — strakes that are thicker than the normal planking — are similar to the stringers running longitudinally on the inside of the frames. The lowest wale, just above the waterline, is 6 inches thick. The next above it is 5 inches thick, while the rest are 3½ inches.

65

So, too, the planking itself varies in thickness. The bottom planking is 2 inches thick; the topmost, 1½ inches. To provide longitudinal strength where it is needed — in the region just above the waterline — the planking between the lower wale and the second wale is a full 3 inches thick. The hull from the keel to the waterline is planked with courbaril, a tropical hardwood. Juniper, a softer wood from the middle Atlantic states, is used above the waterline. The planks are fastened to the frames either with trunnels or spikes or both.

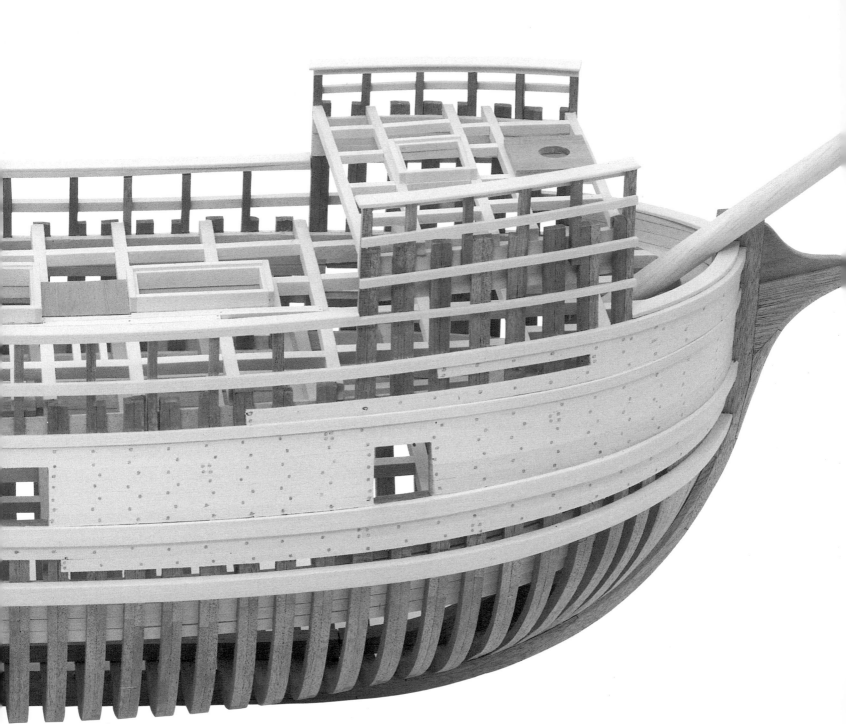

right

The hull planking is almost finished. The shipwrights
have prepared to plank the main deck by fitting the
waterways — thicker planks at the outside margin of
the deck. The waterways are notched and beveled to fit
around the projecting top timbers of the frames, which
here serve as framing for the bulwarks, the high rail
above the deck.

The square opening in the side of the hull is a
gunport, which will be fitted later with a lid. Note the
bevel along the top edge of the thick red channel wale
and the black main wales below the gunport. This is
not a matter of decoration. Rather, the bevel allows
water to drain off the top of the wales and not become
trapped in a corner to cause rot.

Behold at last,
Each tall and tapering mast
Is swung into its place;
Shrouds and stays
Holding it firm and fast!

The three masts of the *Susan Constant* began as trees, giant Douglas firs, in the forest. Carefully selected for their clear, straight grain, they were hewn to the proper diameter and taper in the age-old manner.

To make a mast, the shipwrights first squared the tree along its length in cross section, then tapered it — the mast is thicker in diameter at the bottom than it is at the top — then made it eight-sided, then sixteen-sided, and finally round. As can be imagined, mastmaking requires the eye of an artist and the hand of a craftsman. What's more, it produces an incredible amount of wood shavings and chips.

Once the mast itself has been made, it must be fitted with the accessories that assist in its work. The crossed timbers at the head of this mast are known as the crosstrees and trestletrees; they provide the foundation for the top, a platform for the lookout, and a miniature deck in the sky for the sailors when they work in the rigging. The rectangular piece at the top of the mast is the cap; the round hole in it holds the topmast — a lighter, higher mast that carries the topsail.

The rigging looped around the mast just above the crosstrees and the trestletrees is the standing rigging — shrouds and stays used to support the mast. Shrouds support the mast in a side-to-side direction; stays perform the same function in a fore-and-aft direction.

70

The running rigging, yet to be fitted, generally is lighter than the standing rigging and is used for raising, lowering, and adjusting the sails, as well as for bracing the yards — the long, tapering spars that cross the masts and from which the sails are set.

The seams between the planks are made watertight with caulking, strands of oakum, usually treated with oils as a preservative. Here, the ends of caulking strands have been left hanging to indicate where the caulkers have left off work for the day.

By design, the edges of the planks are not square; rather, they are planed to a slight bevel before being hung, so that two planks, edge-to-edge, will form a V-shaped seam — the back of the seam tight, the front open. The caulkers fill the seam with long strands of rolled oakum, driving it down firmly with a caulking iron — a chisel-shaped tool — that is struck with a heavy mallet. The seam is then covered with a flexible compound, putty, to smooth the surface and hold the caulking in place.

right

The work of the caulker looks simple, but it is a difficult trade to practice, since swinging the mallet, especially in tight spaces near the keel, is wearing on the body. It also requires the right touch: Too much oakum will force the seams apart; too little will produce a leaky seam. The right amount, driven perfectly, not only will keep the water out but also will contribute to the strength of the hull.

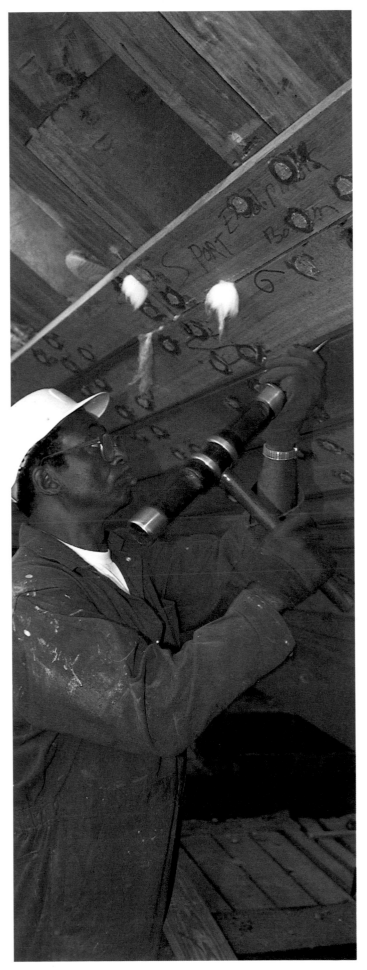

The captain's cabin, yet to be finished, is a study of the massive structure of a wooden ship. Thick vertical knees, called hanging knees, support the quarterdeck framing. Equally heavy horizontal knees, called lodging knees, brace the ends of the deckbeams to the side of the hull. All are bolted securely. The open doors lead to the stern gallery, an outside balcony around the after part of the ship. Much still remains to be done to the interior of the hull in the way of accommodations and storage compartments.

The planking of the lower deck has yet to be laid, but the framing has been completed. Eventually, the joiners — finish carpenters — will build in bunks and other accommodations. The *Susan Constant*, as a lowly merchant ship, was lightly armed, but she nevertheless carried eight guns, all of which were on this deck, sharing space with the crew and passengers.

above
Extra reinforcement is a fact of life on a wooden ship. The pillars help the hanging knees at the side to carry the load of the main deck. Special timbers called partners reinforce the main deck, above, where it is pierced by the mast.

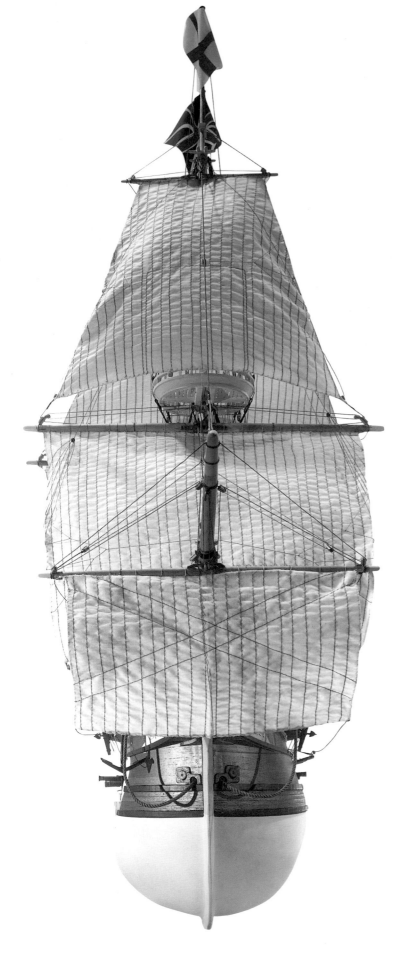

The bottom of a wooden ship must be protected from fouling by sea grass and barnacles and also from boring teredos (shipworms), which in short order can ruin planking the way termites can destroy a house.

Seventeenth-century shipwrights did the best they could, given the knowledge and technology of the time, but their techniques were nowhere nearly as effective as modern methods. A common treatment was to coat

the bottom with tar and animal hair, then sheathe it
with a half- to one-inch layer of thin planking, and
coat that with a white-colored mixture of oil, rosin, and
brimstone — a treatment that was not very effective

against warm-water shipworms. For this reproduction of
the *Susan Constant*, the shipwrights used modern
bottom paint, dark red in color from the presence of
copper in the mixture.

After the hull is closed in, the decks are laid, and the masts are raised comes an incredible amount of detail work. Hardware and fastenings for a ship like the *Susan Constant*, for example, cannot be bought off the shelf; they must be handmade by the shipsmith, a blacksmith who specializes in ship fittings. The steering gear must be made and installed, the stern gallery must be constructed, the interior accommodations must be fitted, and, of course, the hull must be painted.

Considerable research went into determining authentic
paint colors and designs for the hull of the *Susan
Constant*. Clues were found in paintings of period
ships, manuscript illustrations, and an English model
of a similar ship, dating from about 1630.

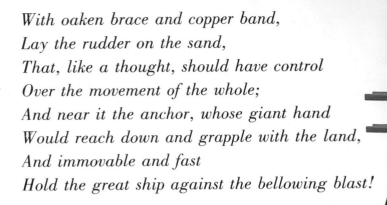

With oaken brace and copper band,
Lay the rudder on the sand,
That, like a thought, should have control
Over the movement of the whole;
And near it the anchor, whose giant hand
Would reach down and grapple with the land,
And immovable and fast
Hold the great ship against the bellowing blast!

On launching day, the only evidence that this is a reproduction, not the original seventeenth-century vessel, is the presence of copper bottom paint and two bronze propellers. The new *Susan Constant* has been fitted with twin engines to increase her range and assist in maneuvering. Sail is nevertheless the principal motive power of this vessel. To prepare for that, two riggers work on the foremast, reeving the running rigging. When they are finished, the masts will support an intricate maze of halyards, sheets, and braces — the lines used to handle the sails — each with a specific purpose.

Then the Master,
With a gesture of command,
Waved his hand;
And at the word,
Loud and sudden there was heard,
All around them and below,
The sound of hammers, blow on blow,
Knocking away the shores and spurs.
And see! she stirs!

She starts, — she moves, — she seems to feel
The thrill of life along her keel,
And, spurning with her foot the ground,
With one exulting, joyous bound,
She leaps into the ocean's arms.

No ship, wooden or otherwise, is launched in a ready-to-sail condition. In fact, most sailing ships were launched without masts and rigging; they were later towed to a fitting-out dock, where sheerlegs, or cranes, were used to step the masts and cross the yards. Much remains to be done following the launch. First, the shipwrights check to see whether the hull floats on her marks — that is, her designed, painted waterline lies horizontal with the water and the hull rests at the proper depth in it. If not, they will add or subtract ballast — dead weight — or move the ballast to make the hull float on her marks. Then they will reeve the necessary rigging, bend on the sails, check the set of the sails and the lead of the running rigging, fit the gun ports (in the photograph above they are covered temporarily with plywood), and prepare the ship for her sea trials.

The sea trials are the first opportunity for the sailing crew to determine how well the designers and shipwrights did their job. The *Susan Constant* sets sail down the James River for the more open water of Chesapeake Bay, where she will be put through her paces in a variety of sea and wind conditions. The captain will sail her off the wind, on the wind, tack her, jibe her, set her sails in various combinations, and in general see how she goes. Then she will be sailed back to Jamestown, where necessary modifications will be made to her hull and rig. Only then will the *Susan Constant* be declared as ready for the sea as was her namesake back in 1607.

Belowdecks, the completed *Susan Constant* is clean
and spare, with ample light and ventilation from the
open main hatch. On an ocean voyage, this space
would be crowded with passengers, crew, hammocks,
supplies, gear, the cannon that make up the vessel's
armament, and more. There would barely be room
enough to move around.

All is shipshape and Bristol fashion on the maiden voyage.

Looking forward along the upper deck. The cook room,
which contains a brick-and-mortar stove and a huge
iron kettle, is entered through the rectangular door of
the forward structure. The mainmast is in the
foreground, with the handle to one of the two main
pumps nearby. In the distance is the bowsprit and the
yard from which the spritsail is set.

Looking aft along the upper deck. In the far
background is the quarterdeck, the domain of the
captain, with the belfry at the forward edge. The
helmsman steers the ship from a little compartment
under the shelter of the quarterdeck. His only view is
through the window just below the belfry. In the
foreground, the barrel structure with spokes is the
capstan, which is used to raise the anchor. Just aft of
the capstan is the main hatch, covered with a grating
to provide sunlight and ventilation below; in foul
weather, it is battened down with a canvas cover.

If the hull of the *Susan Constant* is her body, and the
sails her wings, then the belfry, with the ship's bell
inside, is her soul. The bell is at once the timekeeper
of the watch on deck — the sailors on duty — and the
crew resting below, and the symbol of life on board.
The belfry, then, is like a tabernacle, and the ship a
church.

We are outward bound for the west to-night,
　And the yard goes up with a cheer;
And the bells will ring in the town to-night,
　And the men in the inns will hear.

And the carts will creak in the lanes to-night,
　And the girls will dance to the band;
But we shall be out with the sails to fist,
　And the topsail-sheets to hand.

— Anonymous

The new *Susan Constant*

Keel laid, December 11, 1989
Launched, December 14, 1990
Commissioned, April 26, 1991

Location: Jamestown Settlement, adjacent to Jamestown
National Historic Site, Jamestown, Virginia

Historical research: Brian Lavery, Great Britain
Working plans: Stanley Potter, naval architect,
Beaufort, North Carolina
Master shipbuilder: Allen Rawl, Bradshaw, Maryland

The construction crew of seventy people included such
specialists as shipwrights, plankers, caulkers,
woodcarvers, carpenters, blacksmiths, shipsmiths,
electricians, and machinists.

*Cost: $2.1 million, including research, design,
materials, labor, and construction*

Overall length, 116 feet
Length of hull, 96 feet
Length on deck, 82 feet
Length on waterline, 77 feet
Beam, 24 feet 10 inches
Draft, 11 feet 9 inches
Height of mainmast from waterline, 95 feet
Sail area, 3,902 square feet
Displacement, 275 tons
Net tonnage, 120
Ballast, 110 tons of lead
Auxiliary power, two 135-horsepower diesel engines

Materials
Keel: greenheart
Frame: mora, purpleheart, and courbaril
Planking below waterline: courbaril
Planking above waterline: juniper
Deck structure, ceiling, bulkheads, and furniture:
long-leaf yellow pine
Masts and yards: Douglas fir
      About 150,000 board feet of wood were used.

Decoration
Based on that common to other merchant vessels of the
period. The decorations on the gallery and the
beakhead were copied from a ship model of about
1630.

Flags
On the mainmast is the British national flag of the
period, which is the Union Jack combining the English
cross of Saint George with the Scottish cross of Saint
Andrew. On the other two masts are flags with the
cross of Saint George, the symbol of England since the
Middle Ages.

The original James Fort, the main settlement at
Jamestown, was founded in the spring of 1607,
following a long search by the colonists for an
appropriate site. This re-creation at the Jamestown
Settlement, near Williamsburg, Virginia, contains more
than fifteen thatch-roofed structures built in wattle-and-
daub style. Surrounded by a high wooden stockade,
the little village includes homes, a church, a
storehouse, and a guard building.